OFF-CENTERED RIDING
Or
Not So Swift

OFF-CENTERED RIDING
Or
Not So Swift

Illustrated by Ruth Perkins   Introduced by Sally Swift

Trafalgar Square Publishing

NORTH POMFRET, VERMONT

Published by Trafalgar Square Publishing
North Pomfret, Vermont 05053

Library of Congress Cataloging-in-Publication Data

Perkins, Ruth, 1951–
    Off-centered riding : or not so Swift / by Ruth Perkins;
introduced by Sally Swift.
    p. cm.
    ISBN 0–943955–81–5 (pbk.)
    1. Horsemanship—Caricatures and cartoons.
    2. American wit and humor, Pictorial.
    I. Swift, Sally, 1913– Centered riding. II. Title.
NC1429.P397A4   1993
741.5'973–dc20   93–24127
                                  CIP

ACKNOWLEDGMENTS

With great appreciation and thanks to all the people who have helped this book come to print:

To Sally Swift, whose valuable insights and inspirational teachings have made my riding more rewarding and successful...really.

To Patsy Shaffer of Bath, Maine who introduced me to Sally Swift and the Centered Riding techniques. Her patience, laughter, and encouragement inspired me to keep riding and to compile my drawings into this book.

To Caroline Robbins for her tireless efforts to understand my sketches, her skillful comments, and her deft handling of the details involved in the publishing of this book...mostly from long distance!

To Ollie Sewall for "Not So Swift" and to Janet Blevins for insisting that I put the drawings together! To Pat, Marcia, and the crew at Quantico Stables for their hard work and for letting me "experiment" with their horses.

Lastly, a special thanks to all my family, and especially to George, Nate, and Becky for their love and for understanding that horsepeople are just a little bit nuts.

INTRODUCTION

I have often said that if a stranger was to walk into one of my Centered Riding clinics, she would think that she had walked into a madhouse. Ruth Perkins has now proved I was right. These brilliant, delightful, and hysterically funny drawings have had my senior instructors and me virtually rolling on the floor in helpless laughter.

It is important for my students to have some knowledge of anatomy, the functions of their bones and joints, and an awareness of the movement of their bodies. All this together promotes harmony between horse and rider. The use of imagery is also part of my teaching technique. When used appropriately, it can trigger miraculous results—and, hopefully, some relaxing smiles. Now, with this book, we can revel in the purely ridiculous, fun side of these images.

May you have as many laughs as I from Ruth's delightful collection of spoofs.

Sally Swift

PREFACE

The first time I rode in one of Sally Swift's clinics, I was riding an obstinate Appaloosa mare. In the beginning, my mare's "forward walk" was anything but forward. My legs were whacking away at her sides, her ears were laid back and her head was up—a painful sight, at best. Then, with Sally's infinite patience, calming images and amazing insight, my mare miraculously relaxed, lengthened her stride, and even trotted forward with her back round and her nose going toward the ground. Two Centered Riding converts were born that day!

This book was inspired by the many trials and tribulations—even disasters—I experienced as I first attempted to put into practice the techniques and images of Centered Riding.

Later, I spent many moments laughing as I pictured myself in these attempts. However, I found that when I actually put these pictures down on paper, I could often understand what went wrong with my riding that day. The results of my misdirected cues and "not-so-Swift" attempts to teach my body how to respond to Sally's teachings are chronicled in this tribute to Centered Riding.

I have ridden many horses since that first clinic with Sally in 1981, each with a different personality and different eccentricities. I still ride horses who do not want to move forward, horses who move too fast, who are terrified at the sight of a dog or a leaf, and horses who sail over an eighteen-inch-high cross rail as if it was a seven-foot oxer. Sally's book has been my Bible through it all—a calming, sensible influence in my hours of confusion and dismay. Thank you, Sally Swift!

Ruth Perkins

Appeal to the Great Spirit!

Think of riding as a beautiful dance full of motion, aesthetics, coordination and flow.

Start every ride with a quiet period at a walk.

Breathing only in your chest is like blowing up a balloon.

Visualize a bellows between your diaphragm and your pelvis
and quietly keep it opening and shutting.

When you hold your breath, you build certain tensions in your body
to which your horse will react.

If you imagine that you are a doll weighted at the bottom,
you will remain stable.

The building blocks must be carefully balanced.

There is a plumbline hanging from your ear. It should go through your center.

Feel a spring pulling your center forward toward the sky.

When you concentrate, distractions are of no concern.

Learning to "ride with your bones" can be a bit frightening at first.

Imagine that the tops of your legs are mobile flippers extending out from the pelvis. This can produce surprising results!

To let the head go properly forward and up,
imagine some hair being tugged from the top of your head.

As you ride, pretend your head is a billiard ball and you are balancing it
on the end of a pool cue.

Imagine that you send the weight out of your heavy, strong leg
and drop it into the light, weak leg.

Be a spruce tree.
The roots grow down from your center as the trunk grows up.

Ride with your stubby legs.

Allow dried sand to spill out of the bottom of your boots.

Imagine that your legs are so long that your feet rest on the ground.

Think of a ship's mast going up through your body,
with your shoulders and arms as the yardarm.

Your forearm should reach from elbow to bit.

Pretend that your arms and hands are soft garden hoses.

Strict obedience must be acquired through repeated, appropriate work—
you must lead the way.

Remember: the conversation between you and your horse
must never be dull or inert.

At a canter, the horse's back moves like a seesaw. Your hips must open and close with this motion.

When cantering, remember the reverse monkey.

Using your *ki* to stop your horse, imagine dropping a heavy chain into the ground to anchor him there.

Imagine that the energy from the horse's inside hind foot and your inside leg will bounce against and off the outside rein like a tennis ball against a backboard.

Think of the contained energy as a slinky toy—
a flexible spring with coils that bounce back and forth.

Imagine a diagonal line of energy streaming up through your body
like a laser beam or a rocket.

Visualize a powerful wind lifting up you and your horse.
You will fly effortlessly, scarcely touching the ground.

Feel that your center is going to fly out between your hands.

Blow your horse forward with puffs of breath.

Send your horse forward from your legs,
like squeezing toothpaste out of a tube.

While jumping, bring your center near the pommel,
where you will quietly remain during the flight.

Pretend that your feet are flat on the ground and just skate over the jumps.

To help with your breathing, try singing your way over a jumping course.

The horse becomes a well-oiled steam engine moving strongly, pulsating, with all the joints and pistons working fully.

The result of the centered approach to riding:
Your dream ride will come true.

BIOGRAPHY

Ruth Perkins was born and raised in New York City and Connecticut. She has been interested in drawing since she was three years old, when she created her first mural on the hallway wall. She has since gone on to design and paint murals for hospitals, day-care centers and businesses, and, in addition, she has worked as a medical illustrator and on advertising campaigns. She is currently teaching art as well as schooling horses for the Marine base stable at Quantico, Virginia. Ruth is married, has two children, one Thoroughbred mare and two cats.